This book is dedicated to our twins.
They inspired this story.

Caleb and Mr. Billy BandAid are best friends. They love to play at the park.

CALEB HURT HIMSELF WHILE
PLAYING ON THE TIRE SWING TODAY.

CALEB'S MOM SAID THAT IT'S TIME
TO GO GET HIS KNEE CHECKED AT
THE MEDICAL CLINIC.

CALEB IS SCARED TO GO TO THE MEDICAL CLINIC.

MR. BILLY BANDAID HUGS CALEB
AND TELLS HIM THAT THE
MEDICAL CLINIC ISN'T SCARY. IT'S
FUN AND CAN HELP YOU FEEL
BETTER.

CALEB ASKS MR. BILLY BANDAID,
"DO I HAVE TO GET A BOO-
BOO?"

MR. BILLY BANDAID TELLS CALEB THAT
HE MAY HAVE TO GET A BOO-BOO,
BUT ITS OK.

YOU CAN GET A BANDAID, ONE OF MY
FRIENDS....MAYBE EVEN A SUPER
HERO STICKER AND A LOLLIPOP.

WE ARE HERE AT THE CLINIC CALEB.

Medical Clinic

KNOCK KNOCK.....

IT'S MS. ISABELLA, THE NURSE
PRACTITIONER. SHE'S HERE TO
TAKE CARE OF CALEB.

MS. ISABELLA IS SO NICE AND
SHE CHECKED MY KNEE AND
CLEANED IT ALL UP. I WAS
WORRIED ABOUT A SHOT AND
DIDN'T EVEN HAVE TO GET
ONE.. SHE MADE ME FEEL SO
MUCH BETTER.

HEY CALEB.....HAVING A CHECK-UP
ISN'T SO BAD AFTER ALL?

THE END

Made in the USA
Lexington, KY
21 September 2019